Student
DISCUSSION GUIDE

t o

The Call of the Wild

By Nancy Romero

Talent Development Secondary Publications
Center for Social Organization of Schools
Johns Hopkins University
Baltimore

Discussion Guide #1

Chapters 1 and 2

Vocabulary List A

paddocks (p.3)	deft (p. 5)	parched (adj., p. 8)
imperiously (p. 3)	*futilely (p. 5)	metamorphosed (p. 9)
sated (p. 3)	vilely (p. 5)	
aristocrat (p. 3)	ebbed (p. 5)	fiend (p. 9)
trifle (adv., p. 3)	*intolerable (p. 6)	gingerly (p. 9)
*egotistical (p. 3)	*impending (p. 7)	uncowed (p. 12)
insular (p. 3)	calamity (p. 7)	conciliated (p. 13)
pampered (adj., p. 3)	unkempt p. 7)	uncouth (p. 13)
progeny (p. 4)	*taunted (v., p. 8)	wheedlingly (p. 13)
rage (n., p. 5)	waxed (p. 8)	swarthy (p. 14)

Special Glossary

artesian well - a kind of well built so that groundwater flows upwards out of a well without the need for pumping.

demesne - a large piece of land owned by one person; an estate

pent - penned; held or kept in

Santa Clara Valley - an area in Western California near the city of San Jose

Puget Sound - an inlet off the ocean that lies off the coast of the state of Washington

Arctic - the region around the North Pole

Northland - a term used by Jack London to refer to the cold, harsh region north of the continental United States

Klondike strike - reference to the gold rush that occurred in the 1800s in the Klondike region of Canada near the Alaskan border

hydrophoby - a disease potentially fatal to humans that is spread by bites from infected animals, also known as rabies

sacredam - a mild French Canadian curse word

Southland - a term used by Jack London to refer to Buck's home-land, the region south of the Alaskan and Canadian borders

continued on page 2

dispatches - official messages or mail

Geological Survey - government organization that studies the environment

the Barrens - a vast, frozen area in northern Canada where few plants grow

Queen Charlotte Sound - a deep, wide inlet off the Pacific Ocean that lies off the coast of western Canada

 The Writer's Craft

Figurative Language

Characterization is the way an author develops characters so that readers can picture them and understand their feelings and actions. An author can give readers descriptions of characters, or use characters' words, actions, or thoughts to help them learn what the characters are like. The characterization in *The Call of the Wild* is unusual because the main character, Buck, is a dog. Think about Jack London's characterization of Buck as you read the first chapter of the novel. Consider the kinds of words or phrases you would use to describe Buck's character. Do you think Buck acts and thinks more like a dog or like a human?

DISCUSSION QUESTIONS AND ACTIVITIES

Section I. Read chapter 1 (pages 1-16). Discuss your responses to the questions and activities with a classmate. Then write your answers independently.

1. **Why is Buck sold? Why are Buck and other dogs like him in demand along the Pacific Coast?**

_____

_____

_____

_____

_____

_____

_____

_____

2. **Why is Buck shocked by the treatment he receives after he is sold? What unforgettable lesson does "the club" teach him?**

_____

_____

_____

_____

_____

_____

_____

3. **Describe both Buck's human- and dog-like qualities.**

_____

_____

_____

_____

_____

_____

4. **Who are Francois and Perrault, and why does Buck respect them?**

_____

_____

_____

_____

_____

_____

5. **What shows that Buck is already beginning to adapt to his new surroundings?**

_____

_____

_____

_____

_____

_____

_____

Make A
Prediction:

How will Buck cope in his new life in the harsh Arctic?

How will all of the dogs owned by Francois and Perrault interact with one another?

What other lessons will Buck learn?

Vocabulary List B

imperative (adj., p. 17)	belligerent (p. 20)	animated (p. 24)
vicarious (p. 17)	ignominiously (p. 21)	retaliate (p. 25)
draught (p. 19)	forlorn (p. 22)	routed (p. 26)
*perpetual (p. 20)	spasmodically (p. 23)	fastidiousness (p. 27)
*malignant (p. 20)	arduous (p. 23)	*callous (adj., p. 28)
incarnation (p. 20)	placatingly (p. 23)	*conspicuous (p. 29)
prowess (p. 20)	*despise (p. 24)	leeward (p. 29)

Special Glossary

primordial - primitive; that which has existed from the beginning

civilization - social organization of a higher order, marked by such things as the development of a written language, the arts and sciences, government, etc.

moral nature - the ability to tell the difference between right and wrong

 The Writer's Craft

Contrast

Contrast occurs when an opposing idea or thing is presented for the sake of emphasis or clearness. Jack London uses contrast often in the beginning of *The Call of the Wild*. In the first chapter, London contrasts Buck's earlier lifestyle in the Southland with his new lifestyle in the Northland. As you read chapter 2, notice how London further develops this contrast. Why do you think he does this?

DISCUSSION QUESTIONS AND ACTIVITIES

Section II. Read chapter 2 (pages 17-30). Discuss answers to the following questions with a classmate, then write your answers independently.

1. **What does Buck learn from Curly's death? How does Curly's death change Buck's relationship with Spitz?**

_____

_____

_____

_____

_____

_____

2. **What is "the law of the club and the fang," the law followed by both dogs and men in the Northland? What incidents have taught this law to Buck?**

_____

_____

_____

_____

_____

_____

_____

3. **Contrast life in the Southland with life in the Northland. How has Buck changed to adapt to his new life in the Northland?**

_____

_____

_____

_____

_____

_____

_____

4. **London compares the contrast between the Southland and the Northland with the contrast between civilization and "things primordial." What is London trying to communicate through this comparison?**

_____

_____

_____

_____

_____

_____

5. **Why has Buck's adaptation to the hostile environment of the Northland been easy and rapid?**

_____

_____

_____

_____

_____

_____

Make A
Prediction:

**What new problems
will Buck encounter
as he continues to
travel through the
Northland?**

Literature-Related Writing

1. If Buck could write a **letter** to his former owner, Judge Miller, about his new life in the Northland, what would he write? Would he express a desire to return to the Southland or not? Write a letter from Buck to Judge Miller expressing his thoughts.

2. Write a **poem** that describes the "law of the club and the fang."

3. Pretend you are an animal rights activist living during the time of the Klondike gold rush. Write an **editorial** about the treatment of sled dogs used by the men searching for gold.

 Extension Activities

1. Draw two contrasting pictures—one depicting life for Buck in the Santa Clara Valley and another depicting life in the frozen Northland.

2. Research the Klondike-region gold rush of the late 1800s. Share what you learn with your classmates.

Discussion Guide #2

Chapters 3 and 4

Vocabulary List A

*dominant (p. 31)
cunning (n., p. 31)
poise (n., p. 31)
pandemonium (p. 33)
skulking (p. 33)
malingerer (p. 34)
adversary (p. 34)
din (p. 34)

jugular (n., p. 34)
*daunted (p. 36)
dubiously (p. 36)
*defied (p. 36)
*shirked (p. 41)
prostrate (adj., p. 41)
abjectly (p. 41)
covert (p. 42)

insubordination (p. 42)
insidious (p. 44)
*rampant (p. 47)
exultantly (p. 49)
inexorable (p. 50)

Special Glossary

score - twenty people or things

eddies - small whirlpools

aurora borealis - streamer-like colored lights seen in the sky near the North Pole; also known as the Northern Lights

 The Writer's Craft

Figurative Language

Jack London uses **figurative language** often in *The Call of the Wild*. Figurative language is language used to describe by means of comparisons. A **simile** is a comparison introduced by "like" or "as," for example, "Joe was snapping like a demon" (p. 34). In this simile, Joe's behavior is compared to that of a demon. Like the simile, the **metaphor** compares two things, but it does not contain the words

continued...

"like" or "as." It states or implies that one thing is another. For example, "...and Toots and Ysabel [Buck] utterly ignored, for he was king... (p. 3). In this metaphor, Buck is called a king because this is how he views himself. He ignores the other dogs because he considers them less important than himself.

Personification is the giving of human attributes to an animal or an object. For example, the statement, "My hair never obeys me," is personification because the hair is described as having a human characteristic, the ability to disobey. As you read the following section, look for more examples of these types of figurative language.

DISCUSSION QUESTIONS AND ACTIVITIES

Section I. Read chapter 3 (pages 31-51). Discuss answers to the following questions with a classmate, then write your answers independently.

1. **A major theme in this novel is the fight for survival. List several incidents in chapter 3 that bring out this theme.**

_____

_____

_____

_____

_____

_____

_____

2. **According to the narrator, what does Buck learn from the red-sweatered man that makes him so dangerous?**

_____

_____

_____

_____

_____

_____

3. **How does Buck and Spitz's battle for leadership affect the dog sled team?**

_____

_____

_____

_____

_____

_____

_____

_____

4. **Although Spitz is a much more experienced fighter, Buck is able to defeat him. Why is Buck able to kill Spitz?**

_____

_____

_____

_____

_____

_____

5. **What descriptions in this chapter show that Buck has become completely primitive?**

_____

_____

_____

_____

_____

_____

_____

Make A
Prediction:

Will the dogsled team respond to Spitz's death? Will the dogs continue to cause trouble for Francois and Perrault?

Vocabulary List B

*coveted (adj., p. 52)   celerity (p. 56)   suppressedly (p. 61)

obdurate (p. 53)   *monotonous (p. 58)   lugubriously (p. 63)

forevalued (p. 54)   *potent (p. 59)

*sheepishly (p. 54)   resiliency (p. 60)

Special Glossary

Scotch - of or about the country of Scotland (usually "Scottish")

half-breed - a rude term for a person whose parents are of different ethnic groups

DISCUSSION QUESTIONS AND ACTIVITIES

Section II. Read chapter 4 (pages 52-65). Discuss answers to the following questions with a classmate, then write your answers independently.

1. **Buck conquered "the law of the fang" in his cunning and savage defeat of Spitz. How does he conquer the "law of the club" in this chapter?**

_____

_____

_____

_____

_____

_____

2. **What kind of leader is Buck?**

_____

_____

_____

_____

_____

_____

3. **What do you learn about Buck from his dreams?**

_____

_____

_____

_____

_____

_____

4. **Why do the men harness Dave with the team, although he is clearly dying?**

_____

_____

_____

_____

_____

_____

Make A
Prediction:

**Buck has conquered
his enemy, Spitz, and
has overcome many
difficulties to take
over the leadership
of the dog team.
Predict Buck's next
challenge.**

Literature-Related Writing

1. An **epitaph** is a saying written on a tomb or gravestone in memory of the person buried there. Write epitaphs for both Spitz's and Dave's tombstones. Make the epitaphs reflect their characters and lives.

2. Pretend that the Canadian government needs more dispatchers to perform work similar to that of Francois and Perrault. Write a **classified advertisement** for a Canadian newspaper describing the job. Describe the job's challenges and benefits.

3. Buck's Northland environment is governed by the law of the club and the fang. He has learned how to survive in the context of these laws. Give a name to the "law" under which you must live. Describe this **law** and explain how you have learned to live with it.

 Extension Activities

1. Do research on dog sledding. How does today's dog sledding compare and contrast to the dog sledding described in *The Call of the Wild*? Is dog sledding still used for work or only for sport? Tell your classmates what you learn from your research.

2. Draw a scene from one of Buck's dreams.

3. Design a book cover for *The Call of the Wild* that reflects its survival theme.

4. Create symbols to represent the law of the fang and the law of the club.

Discussion Guide #3

Chapters 5 and 6

Vocabulary List A

*feigned (p. 66)
fatigue (n., p. 66)
*taut (p. 67)
salient (p. 68)
callowness (p. 68)
unutterable (p. 68)
slovenly (p. 68)
repugnance (p. 70)

clannish (p. 71)
superfluous (p. 73)
*discarded (adj., p. 73)
averred (p. 73)
famine (p. 77)
voracious (p. 77)
copious (p. 80)

prerogative (p. 80)
perambulating (p. 82)
wayfarers (p. 84)
innocuously (p. 84)
terse (p. 84)
impending (p. 86)
*inarticulate (p. 86)
*chaotic (p. 87)

Special Glossary

mongrels - mixed-breeds

fissures - long, deep cracks

 The Writer's Craft

Foreshadowing and *Alliteration*

Foreshadowing occurs in a story when the author gives clues about events yet to come. As you read the beginning of chapter 5, watch for these kinds of hints. Make a prediction about what will happen later in the chapter.

Alliteration is the repetition of an initial consonant sound, as in "**r**ough and **r**eady" and "**sl**owing **sl**ipping." Alliteration is often used in poetry. Alliteration produces a pleasing sound, and phrases containing alliteration are especially enjoyable when read out loud. The following chapter contains many examples of alliteration. See if you can find them, and say the phrases out loud.

DISCUSSION QUESTIONS AND ACTIVITIES

Section I. Read chapter 5 (pages 66-88). Discuss answers to the following questions with a classmate, then write your answers independently.

1. **What hints at the beginning of the chapter *foreshadow* that Buck's new journey will be a tragic one?**

_____

_____

_____

_____

_____

_____

2. **Describe Buck's new owners, Hal, Charles, and Mercedes. How do they contrast with Buck's former owners in the Northland?**

_____

_____

_____

_____

_____

_____

3. **Several new dogs from the Southland are added to Buck's team. They become spirit-broken because they cannot handle their ill-treatment or harsh new environment. Buck, however, was able to rise above similar circumstances when he first arrived in the Northland and become an outstanding contributor to his dog team. What qualities make Buck different from these other dogs? Explain your answer**

_____

_____

_____

_____

_____

_____

_____

_____

4. **How does the spring weather contrast with what is happening among the dogs and their owners?**

_____

_____

_____

_____

_____

_____

5. **How does Buck show he is wiser and more fit for survival than Charles, Hal, and Mercedes?**

_____

_____

_____

_____

_____

_____

_____

Make A
Prediction:

Will Buck stay with John Thornton? What will his life be like now?

Vocabulary List B

demonstrative (p. 90)   peremptorily (p. 94)   repose (n., p. 104)
convalescence (p. 90)   *uncanny (p. 96)   *vigor (p. 104)
*pompous (p. 90)   extremity (p. 100)   conjuration (p. 105)
caress (n., p. 91)   *exploit (n., p. 101)   *incoherent (p. 107)
transient (p. 92)   contagion (p. 104)   babel (p. 107)
wiliness (p. 93)   virility (p. 104)   indiscreet (p. 108)

Special Glossary

tenderfoot - a newcomer who is not used to the hardship associated with the work or the area

totem pole - a pole created by some northwest coastal Indian tribes; it contained carvings of animals and symbols that told memorable stories about tribal people and events.

DISCUSSION QUESTIONS AND ACTIVITIES

Section II. Read chapter 6 (pages 89-108). Discuss answers to the following questions with a classmate, then write your answers independently.

1. **What does Buck experience for the first time in John Thornton's camp?**

_____

_____

_____

_____

_____

_____

2. **How has Buck become famous throughout Alaska?**

_____

_____

_____

_____

_____

_____

3. **What is the call that Buck begins to hear? How does Buck's relationship with John Thornton affect how he responds to the call?**

_____

_____

_____

_____

_____

_____

_____

_____

Make A
Prediction:

Will Buck eventually listen to "the call of the wild," or will he remain attached to the civilized world? Predict the story's ending.

Literature-Related Writing

1. Write a **news article** for an Alaskan newspaper that features the famous dog Buck.

2. Write a **ballad**, a poem or song that tells a story, about Hal, Charles, and Mercedes' experience in the Northland.

3. Write a **letter** of advice from Buck to a group of dogs that have just arrived in the Northland on how to cope in their new environment.

4. Write a **skit** about Hal, Charles, and Mercedes' trip. Perform it for your classmates.

 Extension Activities

1. Learn more about totem poles. Create a small totem pole of symbols that represent memorable events in your own life.

2. Draw a picture of springtime in the Northland as it is described in chapter 5.

3. Research Charles Darwin's concept of the "survival of the fittest." Find out how this concept is used in *The Call of the Wild.* Share what you learn with your classmates.

Discussion Guide #4

Chapter 7

Vocabulary List

melancholy (adj., p. 111)	*coy (p. 116)	palpitant (p. 124)
obliterated (p. 111)	belie (p. 116)	certitude (p. 125)
salient (p. 112)	lope (n., p. 118)	*calamity (p. 125)
subdued (p. 114)	infinitesimal (p. 120)	*stealthily (p. 125)
truce (p. 115)	wantonness (p. 121)	excrescence (p. 126)
commingled (p. 115)	*formidable (p. 121)	*usurp (p. 126)
pertinacity (p. 116)	paroxysms (p. 122)	sluice (adj., p. 128)
	ambuscade (p. 122)	discomfited (p. 131)

 The Writer's Craft

Symbolism

A **symbol** is a real thing used to represent an idea. Examples of symbols include our nation's use of the bald eagle to represent American freedom, a dove used to represent peace, and the seasons spring and winter to represent youth and old age. Symbolism in literature can also be present when a word is used to represent an idea that goes beyond the meaning of the word. For example, the color yellow might be used to represent cowardice in a novel, or the color black might be used to represent death.

Writers often use or create symbols, and the alert reader will watch for them as he or she reads. The repeated use of an object, idea, action, etc., is a hint that it is being used symbolically. Often the reader may have the sense that something written in the story could have a meaning beyond its literal meaning. When the reader senses this, he or she should look for clues in the story that support that possibility.

continued...

In *The Call of the Wild*, author Jack London has created several symbols to represent the primitive life. These have been used over and over throughout the novel and should not be too difficult to identify. Many of these symbols appear in the story's final chapter. Watch for them as you read.

DISCUSSION QUESTIONS AND ACTIVITIES

Read chapter 7 (pages 109-134). Discuss answers to the following questions with a classmate, then write your answers independently.

1. **What symbols used in chapter 7 are also used throughout the novel as representations of the primitive life?**

_____

_____

_____

_____

_____

_____

_____

2. **How are Buck's hunting strategies and skills emphasized in this chapter? What is the author trying to say about Buck by emphasizing these things?**

_____

_____

_____

_____

_____

_____

3. **How does the moose herd respond to Buck's pursuit of their bull leader? How does their response relate to the message of survival in this story?**

_____

_____

_____

_____

_____

_____

_____

4. **To a certain degree, John Thornton and Buck are similar characters and have led similar lives. List these similarities.**

_____

_____

_____

_____

_____

_____

_____

5. **Why does Buck kill the Yeehat Indians? Why does he take great pride in his action?**

_____

_____

_____

_____

_____

_____

_____

Literature-Related Writing

1. Write your own Indian **legend** about Buck.

2. Create your own **symbol** of the wild. Write a descriptive paragraph using the symbol.

3. Write a **poem** that reflects Jack London's perspective on survival and the importance of primitive instincts.

 Extension Activities

1. Depict the "call of the wild" in a drawing or painting.

2. Research wolves. Find out how true wolf behavior compares and contrasts with the wolf behavior described in this novel. Share what you learn with your classmates.

3. One reason that *The Call of the Wild* has been a popular book is because of its setting in the beautiful Alaskan wilderness. Jack London lived there and was able to bring its scenes alive to the reader. Choose an unusual and appealing setting for a novel. Describe the setting and explain why you believe it would be appealing to readers.

ABOUT THE AUTHOR

Jack London was born in 1875 in a poverty-stricken area in Oakland, California. London was born out of wedlock and never knew his true father. London had a difficult childhood, and by age 15 he was a sailor bound for Japan and the Siberian coast. When he returned to the United States, he lived as a vagrant until he decided to enroll in college to further his education. As a student at the University of California, London became interested in politics and writing. He was concerned about the mistreatment of poor, working people. He was also interested in socialism and Charles Darwin's theory of evolution.

Jack London was a traveler, and his journeys took him to the Alaskan wilderness at the time of the Alaskan gold rush. This experience provided the setting for many of London's novels, including his most famous, *The Call of the Wild*. This novel, published in 1902, was one of London's first and brought him instant acclaim and fame. He became one of the most popular and successful writers of his day. London was plagued by numerous health problems, however. He became dependent on the drugs that he took for his pain. He died from an overdose of drugs at the age of forty, an overdose that many believe was intentional.

 SO, YOU WANT TO READ MORE

If you enjoyed *The Call of the Wild*, you may want to read its companion novel, *White Fang*. Also written by Jack London, *White Fang* tells the story of a wild Northland dog that becomes civilized.

Other wilderness adventure stories are Gary Paulsen's *Hatchet*, Armstrong Sperry's *Call It Courage*, Theodore Taylor's *The Cay*, and Scott O'Dell's *The Island of the Blue Dolphins*. *The Adventures of Huckleberry Finn* by Mark Twain and *Treasure Island* by Robert Louis Stevenson are classic adventure stories.

Made in the USA
Coppell, TX
10 August 2022

81218978R00020